A

3rd

Letter to

America

A Spiritual Warning To America

John A. Alexander

To learn more about John's work, upcoming releases, and exclusive updates, please visit:
www.bestsellersbyjohnaalexander.com

For direct contact:
author@bestsellersbyjohnaalexander.com

Published by

Ultra Publishers
www.ultrapublishers.com

Printed in the United States of America

Dedication

After extensive research and hard work devoted to making this book the best it can be, I want to acknowledge that inspiration came easily—because so much information was available. However, the most important inspiration behind every book I write is my family.

They support me fully and trust the message I share through my work. For that reason, I dedicate this book to them—my loving wife and my three wonderful sons.

And above all, to You, my God: You are my everything. My life is lived for You alone. Thank You.

Acknowledgment

We live in a world where we face both good and evil more clearly and intensely than ever before. We see this in the United States during the Trump administration, but it is happening all over the world—in politics, governments, churches, companies, and society as a whole.

The reason I write these books is to help people see that common sense must return to our societies. We cannot continue to endorse individuals, politicians, or institutions when we clearly see evil acts taking place—attacks on truth and attacks on what is right. The warning is simple: if you participate in wrongdoing, you are contributing to the destruction of your nation and the future of the next generation—your children. But if you do your own research, seek truth, and stand for what is right, you become part of building a nation that is blessed and prosperous. In doing so, you help create a better future—one from which your children and loved ones will benefit most. That may become your greatest legacy.

I have three wonderful sons, and I am deeply concerned for them. They need God, solid education, and the ability to see reality clearly—not to be deceived by social media or networks that have shifted far from truth. They must learn to discern lies from truth and resist the evil narratives that are so widely spread today.

I wrote this book as an outsider—I am not American and do not live in the United States—after witnessing years of what I believe to be complete nonsense. Administrations were attacked for securing the border, yet little was said when borders were left open and millions were allowed to enter unchecked. Many of those decisions led to crime, and countless families suffered the loss of children to murder, rape, and other violent acts committed against innocent Americans.

I understand what it means to be attacked for doing what is right and for standing up for truth. For that reason, I was amazed by how President Donald J. Trump stood firm against relentless attacks meant to bring him down. One of the greatest miracles for anyone in such a position is to remain standing—to refuse to compromise standards under pressure. That is why I write these books: so that readers might move from being victims of misinformation to discovering truth, because truth brings freedom.

My hope is that we learn a powerful lesson—that those we attempt to destroy today may one day stand in positions of authority, not seeking revenge, but delivering justice to those who once abused their power.

I hope you enjoy this book.

About the Author

John has traveled extensively around the world, teaching and speaking to companies and religious organizations on topics that remain deeply relevant today. His lectures span a wide range of subjects—from business and politics to personal development, sales, leadership, and marriage—all with a consistent purpose: to challenge his audience to think critically, grow confidently, and strive to become better individuals in every area of life.

With more than forty years of experience influencing and inspiring people face-to-face, John is now embracing a lifelong passion—writing. Through his books, he seeks to share the lessons, insights, and wisdom he has gained over decades of teaching, leadership, and global experience.

He plans to publish four to five books each year, ensuring this is only the beginning of what readers can expect from him. John's knowledge is profound, thought-provoking, and always grounded in truth.

Table of Contents

INTRODUCTION

Blessed is the nation whose God is the Lord

Psalm 33:12 (King James Version)

This is a topic that needs to be spoken about, and why is that?

The scriptures tell us that many have a form of godliness but deny the power, meaning they talk the talk and even do the works, but it is just a form of godliness. Of course, many people are in the place where God is their everything, but we are not talking about them; we are talking about those who appear to be religious, who even pray, but whose lives and hearts are far from where God wants them to be.

America Has Fallen Spiritually

This is not judging a nation or people, but a warning, and we know it's real because it makes sense and is the truth. The word of God is full of warnings, calling people to turn from their ways to God's ways; we call it REPENTANCE, a word no longer received in many churches or one that is afraid to be preached about.

As mentioned, we pray, and we might even quote Scripture, but our hearts are often far from a holy life, a life pleasing unto God.

One of the scariest Scriptures to me in the Bible is, **"There's a way that seems right unto man, but the end is death."** That is frightening; it means people could live their entire lives thinking they were right, only to discover at the end that they were completely wrong about what they believed, spending all those years on earth without seeking the truth of the life to come.

The Bible also says, **"My people perish for lack of knowledge."** Imagine learning how to live on earth but not taking the time to learn how to make it to heaven. This is the reason for this book: a warning to all faiths, religions, and denominations to seek the truth of God's Word and obey it, no matter what.

In John 8, we see a powerful story in which Jesus asks individuals, supposed believers, **"Why are you trying to kill Me for telling you the TRUTH?"** Their response was, **"We are from Abraham's seed."** In today's world, they might say, *"We are Christians, followers of Jesus."* But Jesus answered, **"If you were Abraham's seed, you would act like him."**

Then they said, **"Our Father is Jehovah."** Jesus replied that if Jehovah were truly their Father, they would know who He was. Instead, He declared, **"Your father is the devil."**

WOW, what a rebuke. A rebuke that is still needed in our lives today. Why? Because we must understand that the battle was never merely against a man, but against what that man carried, the **WORD OF GOD**. They hated Jesus because of the Word He carried, and that is the same battle we are facing today in America and all over the world.

If Jesus were to come under a different name today, He would not be received well in most churches. He would expose sin in our midst. He would reveal the wrong we are doing and the false gospels we are preaching that lead people straight to destruction. Churches would reject Him and crucify Him again. Denominations would label Him a troublemaker, and He would have great difficulty fitting into many churches in the world we live in today.

Remember in Revelation 3:20, He is knocking at the door, why? Because He was rejected and kicked out. He is knocking at the doors of many of our churches, saying, **"Will you let Me in?"**, or better yet, **"Will you let Me in again?"**

Many of our churches are no longer the house of God; they have become the house of man. In other words, man dictates what goes on in those churches. We do not have to look far to see this, churches like that are close to us everywhere, showing no sign that the Holy Spirit is in their midst.

I will dedicate one chapter in this book titled **"How to Know if the Holy Spirit Is in Your Life, in Your Home, and in Your Church, or Taking It Further, in Your City/Country?"** We will be shocked to discover the truth. We will find out how far we have fallen from where Jesus wants us to be.

You see, **TRUTH** brings the light of God to us. The light shines and allows us to see the sin within us. Then we must make a choice: do we accept it, or do we reject it?

When Jesus is in our midst, the light shines, and this should be the result:

Isaiah 6:5 , New King James Version

"Woe is me, for I am undone!

Because I am a man of unclean lips,

And I dwell in the midst of a people of unclean lips;

For my eyes have seen the King,

The Lord of hosts."

The glory shone upon him, and he responded to that glory. That glory allowed him to see the real him.

We live in a world today where we pray for the glory, for revival, and for a move of God. But the question is, "Are you ready for His glory to shine and expose your sin, your carnality, your pride, your jealousy, and your wrong doctrine or gospel?" The Word says:

Amos 4:12, New King James Version

"Therefore, thus will I do to you, O Israel;

Because I will do this to you,

Prepare to meet your God, O Israel!"

This is what God says: He has sent warning after warning, but His people have not heeded them and have remained unchanged. They refused to turn from their ways and stayed the same, untouched by His Spirit.

Let us look at a Scripture in Ezekiel:

Ezekiel 33:30–33 , New King James Version

Hearing and Not Doing

"As for you, son of man, the children of your people are talking about you beside the walls and in the doors of the houses; and they speak to one another, everyone saying to his brother, 'Please come and hear what the word is that comes from the Lord.'

So they come to you as people do, they sit before you as My people, and they hear your words, but they do not do them; for with their mouth they show much love, but their hearts pursue their own gain.

Indeed, you are to them as a very lovely song of one who has a pleasant voice and can play well on an instrument; for they hear your words, but they do not do them.

And when this comes to pass, surely it will come, then they will know that a prophet has been among them."

Let us break it down…

- "Come and hear the word of the Lord."
- They come to hear God's Word.
- They come AS God's people, not *God's people come*, but they come AS God's people; they look like God's people.
- They hear, but they do not do.
- "With their mouth they show much love, but their hearts pursue their own gain." Scary.
- They love your preaching, you are like a song to their ears.
- "They hear your words, but they do not do them."

- "When this comes to pass, and surely it will come, "

- "They will know that a prophet has been among them."

There is so much in these verses...

THEY COME HEAR THE WORD OF THE LORD. In other words, they go to church, maybe carry a Bible, but they leave UNCHANGED. They do not do the TRUTH they hear.

The danger here is that they become so used to coming to church to hear the Word of God that the Word becomes just music to their ears. Many chew what they hear but never swallow the truth they hear. They come to hear, and then, two days later, they forget what they heard. They never learn to hear the Spirit of God, so they remain in their immaturity.

That is why Paul came to a group of people saying, "O foolish Galatians! Who has bewitched you that you should not obey the truth, before whose eyes Jesus Christ was clearly portrayed among you as crucified?" Galatians 3:1 (New King James Version),

"For everyone who partakes only of milk is unskilled in the word of righteousness, for he is a babe. But solid food belongs to those who are of full age, that is, those who by reason of use have their senses exercised to discern both good and evil." Hebrews 5:13-14 (New King James Version)

7

I speak to pastors today, and their frustration is this: they preach, they teach, but most people go unchanged. Thank God for those who have learned to heed the Word of God and allow the Word of God and the Spirit of God to do what needs to be done in their lives.

And when you preach on heaven and hell, messages people should hear and understand in order to be ready, they call you insensitive, among other names, and they leave for another church where their ears can be tickled rather than seeking to decrease so that Christ may increase in them.

That is the reason many pastors are resigning, quitting, and taking secular jobs, because they are fighting the apathy and complacency in the hearts of a lukewarm people.

In some cases, this situation was created by the pastors themselves. Then the pastor awakens, realizes the mess that was made, and does not have the patience to wait while God works with him to turn the situation around. You see, it is easier to make a mess than to fix it.

Many pastors are merely maintaining, hoping Jesus would come today and get them out of the mess. But if pastors repent for creating that mess and team up with God to fix it, God will help them. However, they would need to go to their congregation and admit what they have allowed, tell them they want to fix it, and say, "Who is willing to work with God and me to correct where we are and help fix what I have allowed?"

Nehemiah said, "Let us rebuild the walls of Jerusalem." And yes, there were people who were not ready to rebuild, but there were those who were willing, and they did.

The problem I see is that many pastors are **NOT** willing to admit the mess they have allowed, whether financial issues, a failure to truly pray and lead the church to become a praying church, or preaching a compromised gospel because they were afraid to "rock the boat" out of fear that people would leave. I see a large percentage of pastors in this situation.

Many hang on to their churches but no longer have the fire they once had. Instead of resigning and allowing new blood to come in to turn the mess into a miracle, they remain past their time, and their churches continue to die spiritually because they are afraid to let go. I know churches where people are waiting for their pastors to leave or resign so someone fresh can come in and turn the situation around.

We MUST seek what is best for the Kingdom of God rather than what is best for ourselves.

If pastors are not willing to admit the mess they have created, they are not fit to be His disciples.

Congregations are a reflection of their leadership. I have a saying: "Do NOT complain about what YOU have allowed."

If the leadership is weak, the congregation will be weak. If the leadership is carnal, the congregation will be carnal. If the leadership does not pray, the congregation will not pray as they should, or even fast.

The Word of God tells us of two types of leadership: the TRUE SHEPHERDS and the HIRELINGS. The true shepherd fights for the sheep, while the other runs away when trouble comes.

The Word of God says, "Return to your first love," the love you once had for God, and "return to your first works," when you were excited about what Jesus did for you and had no shame in telling others what He did for you.

"I am not ashamed of the gospel of the Lord Jesus Christ, for it is the power of God unto salvation."

We Have Fallen To Deceptions, Distractions

It is NOT disinterest, but DISTRACTIONS.

It is not that we are uninterested in doing things God's way, it is that we are distracted.

What are those distractions?

There are many, but let me speak about this one.

Because we do not see God move as described in the Bible, we begin to create something that appears to be a move of God. What are you saying, John?

Yes, let us look at the different movements that have come into our churches. Many of you may stop reading this book right here and choose not to continue. Why? Because this touches a deep nerve in your life, your doctrine and the ways you have embraced. This is a valid rebuke and a correction to ministries and to personal beliefs.

Let us look at the deceptions that have entered the churches and the reasons the Holy Spirit may have walked away, been grieved, no longer feared, or no longer allowed to lead. The

TRUE children of God are those who allow the Holy Spirit to lead them.

One of the main distractions we see is the **prophetic**, ouch! Don't stop reading. Are you willing to let the Holy Spirit speak to you? Maybe there is truth in what follows.

We believe in the prophetic and in prophecies, but many have turned this into a movement where people gather only to prophesy to one another. By doing so, we have destroyed the lives of many because the prophecies given were never sent by God.

What are you saying, John?

We see this in the Bible. God says that so-called prophets prophesied things He never told them to say. That is correct. This ministry is so sensitive that we must be absolutely sure that what we prophesy truly comes from God.

I can say this because I have encountered many people who prophesy to me or to others and cause harm rather than deliver a true "Thus says the Lord." The victims leave churches because none of the things spoken came to pass, and much of what was said never made sense.

I remember someone prophesying to a woman that she would become a great singer, and everyone clapped at that prophecy. Well, that was over 25 years ago, and she is still not singing, and the list goes on and on. But I do not want to write only on this subject. I am trusting the Holy Spirit to speak to those who are either abusing prophecy while their lives are not in line with holy living, or those who truly believe what they are saying is sent by God when it is not. We have a problem.

We have more so-called prophets in one city than in the entire bible put together!!!!

This is a huge problem.

My question is…… Where are the fishers of men?

A world is going to hell, and churches are distracted from the main commission. Are we adding new people to our churches, or are we merely attracting people through false methods of evangelism?

I knew a church that brought people in to be prophesied over while sitting across from them at tables. How far will we continue to fall? Where are the days when we did things God's way and allowed the Holy Spirit to do His work?

I thank God that, in my early years, I experienced Him as we went out into the streets and parks to preach the gospel. We saw hundreds come to Jesus and be placed into churches.

Another time, we teamed up with many churches in the city and formed a follow-up department. We rented a parking lot at a major intersection, set up a stage, and different worship teams from the churches involved took turns each day. We shared testimonies, and different people preached the Word. We saw many come to Jesus. Where have those days gone?

- Preaching on the streets is not the same as it was back then.

- It must be God now, we must seek how God would have us reach our cities.

- Are we baptizing people in water who have never been discipled? Many churches boast about how many people they have baptized in water. I ask some of those churches, *"Where are those you baptized over the past two years?"* You should see their faces, because many of those people are no longer there.

- Do we have schools of discipleship in our churches where we teach people about being ready for God, about living a holy life, about what it means to die daily and pick up the cross daily, and what it means to be a reflection of God as we were created in His image?

Are we basing our Christian life on how many people we feed rather than becoming a people of CHARACTER? Feeding people is good, and community outreach is great, but as we know, we are NOT saved by works. God is looking for CHARACTER, pure hearts toward Him, so that He may show Himself strong through them.

Instead, we turn God's Word toward teaching people how to become millionaires or how to prophesy, but not how to be like Christ. When we become like Christ, we will never fall into wrong gospels or teachings that allow us to think like the world while believing we are right with God.

The wrong in a nation is not solely the government's problem, though they can play a part. The true problem is the hearts of God's people. "Blessed is the nation whose God is the Lord." We point our fingers at others when God is pointing the finger back at us.

The Bible says: "O Israel, thou hast destroyed thyself; but in Me is thy help."

You see, we are complete in HIM. He did all He did to complete us. Now we must do everything He requires of us to receive that completeness, to fully have the mind of Christ, to be fully His, dead to sin and alive in Him.

The Word says:

"Now that we live, let us live unto Him who died and rose again!"

You see, when we learn that truth, we will only live for Him. We will have come to a place in our lives where we know there is no other way. The disciples came to that place. We all have heroes in the Bible, but do we seek to find out what made them *tick*, what made them become who they became? Or do we just like to quote them without seeking to become what they were?

Listen to Paul in James 1:2–4 New King James Version

My brethren, count it all joy when you fall into various trials, knowing that the testing of your faith produces patience. But let patience have its perfect work, that you may be perfect and lack nothing.

Do we seek to be perfect and COMPLETE, or are we seeking to impress people rather than God?

The Holy Spirit spoke to me years ago. I was doing so much for God and thought He was impressed with me. I burned out a couple of times because I was trying so hard to impress God. You see, I was doing things for God, good things, and it was then that the Holy Spirit came to me, and my life was never the same. He said:

"God is not impressed by the things we do for Him, but by the things we do IN Him!!!"

In other words, many of us do more than what He wants us to do. Are you doing more than what He wants you to do, or are you doing what He wants you to do?

You see, many do not take the time to find out what He truly wants. We go and go, busy for Him, busy for His people, but we leave no time for Him.

That is not me anymore. After that moment, I have never burned out again. Now my life is about giving Him 80% of my time, hearing Him, coming from His presence to give His presence to others. I never want to leave my place in Him now.

I can now sing: *I have found a NEW WAY of living; I have found a new love divine.* That song is so true to me now. I have peace. I know He directs my life. I know I am in right standing with HIM. I still have frustrations about what I see, but I have peace knowing I am in His hands.

What a beautiful place to be.

Discipleship

This is what I believe the Lord is speaking to me and wants me to share with the readers.

Years ago, I had the privilege of visiting Cambodia and a church network with about 25 churches, along with many ministries such as human trafficking rescue, drug centers, homelessness outreach, and more. When I met the pastor, I asked him a question that changed my life forever. You see, before that, I had traveled as an evangelist and pastored churches, but I knew I was missing something, and I knew that churches were missing something as well.

My question to him was:

"HOW CAN YOU HAVE 25 CHURCHES AND ALL THESE MINISTRIES WHEN MOST OF THE COUNTRY, PROBABLY WAY OVER 90%, ARE BUDDHISTS?"

He answered, *"Everything we do Monday, Tuesday, Wednesday, Thursday, Friday, Saturday, and Sunday is about DISCIPLING PEOPLE for the work of the ministry (Ephesians 4:11). We train them here, and then we send them to areas where there are no churches, so we plant churches with those whom we have discipled."*

WOW! I said to myself, we have churches that celebrate 100 years, and yet we have not even reached our neighbors, and all we have is that one church. We have canceled Sunday school, Sunday night services, and evangelistic services. In other words, we have gone backwards instead of forwards.

2 Thessalonians 2:3: "Let no one deceive you by any means, for that Day will not come unless the falling away comes first, and the man of sin is revealed, the son of perdition."

To me, there are two types of discipleship: I call them "Soft Discipleship" and "Hard or Deep Discipleship."

Soft Discipleship would be your Sunday school class for new converts, milk, salad, and a bit of meat.

Then you have the other: stronger discipleship, geared for those who have been in church for many years but still cannot handle strong teaching. In this type of discipleship, we learn to have what the disciples had. We learn what it means to be fit to follow Jesus. Here is where we learn to die to self and allow the Holy Spirit to transform us into His image. This is where we allow Jesus, by His Spirit, to teach us, mold us, and break us according to His will, where the clay sits at the center of the potter's wheel and allows Him to make us the people we ought to be.

We ought to listen to a video about the largest underground movement, where people are saved and healed, thousands come to salvation, and many die for their faith. I'm talking about the underground church in Iran. The YouTube video titled "Sheep Among Wolves" is 1 hour and 53 minutes long. It will convict you and allow you to see how on fire you might be for God, or how lukewarm you may be.

You see, when we went on the streets every Saturday, we were over 60 people. We prayed for two hours before we went. We had Bibles, tracts, guitars, banners, and a megaphone. We saw the power of God move mightily. My point here is that half of those who came with us went into ministry, including me. We were disciplined in action. We took it to other countries as well.

That is why, to me, in the year 2025/2026, if I am to make disciples, teaching them to observe, teaching them to be careful of deceptions and distractions, I must dedicate my life to DISCIPLESHIP. God is looking for disciples: those who would follow Him until the end, those who would ENDURE TO THE END, those who would love Him with everything in them and be able to love their neighbors as themselves. Only two commands, but powerful ones. Much is said in them; Jesus knew what He was saying.

Matthew 28:19–20 , New King James Version

Go therefore and make disciples of all the nations, baptizing them in the name of the Father and of the Son and of the Holy Spirit, teaching them to observe all things that I have commanded you; and lo, I am with you always, even to the end of the age." Amen.

Mark 16:15-20 , New King James Version

And He said to them, "Go into all the world and preach the gospel to every creature. He who believes and is baptized will be saved; but he who does not believe will be condemned. And these signs will follow those who believe: In My name they will cast out demons; they will speak with new tongues; they will take up serpents; and if they drink anything deadly, it will by no means hurt them; they will lay hands on the sick, and they will recover."

Teaching Them to Observe (Discipleship)

Matthew 28:20: "Teaching them to observe all things that I have commanded you; and lo, I am with you always, even to the end of the age." Amen.

I made a comment that when we went to the streets, preached the gospel, and saw many saved, discipled, added to the church, and healed, those who came out with us saw all of these things. 50% of them went into ministry, including me. I was their leader, but the only thing I did was obey God and GO INTO THE WORLD AND PREACH THE GOSPEL.

You see, many churches have stopped not only Sunday school and Sunday night services, but also going out. Many only leave the doors open, hoping new people will come in and get saved. But all they might get is an unhappy believer who has decided to leave their church and check your church.

"It is in the Go that the Lord Goes!"

You see, the latter part of that verse says, "AND I WILL BE WITH YOU." When? When you teach them to observe, and they observe because you GO.

Yes, they can observe a preacher. Yes, they can observe people getting saved. But that most likely will not transform them, nor will it ignite a fire in them that lasts for years to come. Mine has lasted for forty years, praise God, not because of what I have done, but because of what I observed after I became a Christian.

I believe it was 1986. I was young and on fire for God, not fully mature, but I saw the power of God in my life and in the lives of others as we took the gospel to the streets. Then I approached the senior pastor and asked if I could take the gospel to Mexico City at the time of the World Cup, and he gave us his blessing..

We took a team of about twenty or so. We prepared a street presentation of the gospel, and we went. Every night, I preached at a large Assemblies of God church.

On one of the days we went to the streets, I saw a young girl sitting near us. She looked very troubled. I approached her and asked her what was happening in her life. She answered that her friend had been killed. I asked how, and she said they were devil worshippers and attended those churches. She explained that her friend had tried to leave them, but the devils inside her stabbed her to death. She also said that she had run away from them.

I asked some of the girls to look after her, pray with her, and invite her to our revival meetings. Her name was Lupita.

One night, as I was preaching, I saw Lupita trying to get into the church. She was grabbing parts of the wall, pulling herself in, while the devils inside her were trying to pull her out. I signaled the girls from our team, and they went to get her and sat her down close to the stage where I was preaching.

In the middle of the service, demons began to manifest and speak with a man's voice. I saw what was happening and signaled the team to take her to the chapel. They did, and I excused myself and followed them.

The chapel was a good size, about the size of a three-bedroom apartment, and it had only one door going in and out. That door was a glass door, so people were able to see inside.

As we began to pray for her and cast those devils out, the young people of the church were watching through the glass door. As they saw the power of God casting those devils out, they began to enter the chapel. They wanted to cast those devils out themselves. You see, they OBSERVED the power of God in action, and that is what I believe the Word of God talks about.

The disciples walked with Jesus, and they observed the power of God in action; their lives were never the same. They became disciples of Christ and did what they saw, even to the point that their shadows healed people.

This is what is missing in our churches today. We are adding, but we are adding believers from other churches. We take them because we want them in our churches, but what are we doing with the gift that God has given to us? Are we hiding it until He comes for us, or do we work the works of God and do what Jesus did?

You see, we all want to do what Jesus did, but we try to do it our way, and that is the reason we fail. So we open ourselves to things that look like a move of God and allow those fruitless programs to keep us in a lukewarm state.

DO YOU WANT TO DO THE WORKS OF GOD? Don't wait for God, God is waiting for you to GO, to disciple believers for the work of the ministry, teaching them that the HOLY SPIRIT did not come to lift up a man, but to lift up JESUS and Him alone. When we do that, only then will He draw all men unto Him.

Are you seeing people getting saved for the first time every week, or are you seeing the same believers getting saved over and over again?

Time to get back to our first love and our first works.

The question we have to ask ourselves is this: are we adding to the church as we should, or are we preaching to the same crowds every week, making them spiritually fat, unable to move, stuck, weak, and vulnerable to the attacks of the enemy?

IS THAT WHAT THIS SHIP WAS CREATED FOR?

When I look at this ship, a WARSHIP, created to destroy, to defend, to win, and to bring VICTORY, instead it is STUCK, rusting, not able to fight anymore, surrendered for destruction, abandoned as no longer effective. It is sad to see this, but many believers are in the same situation.

When God saves you, you become like Him. You carry His name, His blood, His Spirit, His power. The Word of God says, "I HAVE GIVEN YOU POWER OVER ALL THE POWER OF THE ENEMY, AND NOTHING SHALL HARM YOU." This is a powerful scripture. If that scripture were understood and applied, America should be saved, the world should be saved. His Word would go forth in power and would NOT return void, but would accomplish what He desires.

Instead, we have lost ground. We have been pushed back. We have been entertained by things similar to the things of God, a form of godliness, but NO POWER. The real question is, "IS THAT WHAT YOU WERE SAVED FOR?"

I call it prisoners of war, surrendered to the cares of the world, surrendered to trials and tribulations instead of growing in them. We reject the very things that would cause us to grow spiritually, that would cause us to mature.

We need to be born again, free from the prison we are in. We need to call upon Jesus and say, "SAVE US, OH GOD." Forgive us for falling back. Forgive us for leaving that place of prayer, prayer that gives birth to a new generation.

- A generation that embraces holiness.
- A generation that fears God and God alone.
- A generation full of the Holy Spirit.
- A generation on the move.
- A generation that loves God with everything in them.
- A generation fit to walk with Jesus, fit to be His true disciples.

I believe that generation is coming, and I pray that this book would once again ignite a passion for God, our Lord, our Saviour,

our Deliverer, our Healer, the love of our lives, our Redeemer, our everything.

Let us go to what I believe the Lord showed me years ago about revival.

Why Revival Ended on Many Occasions?

Before we dig into why many revivals didn't last, let us first go to my observations in today's world (2026–2027).

I see many churches claiming that God told them a revival is coming to their church. Others claim revival is coming to their nation, and so on. It is great to believe such things, but if we truly believe that, then my question is this: What are you doing to be ready for that revival?

I remember going to two ministries where they asked me, "Are you the one bringing revival to our region?" I actually smiled when asked, but I never answered at that moment. My answer came through my teachings and preachings, answers that leadership was not ready to receive. The church tripled in size, but leadership was expecting a different type of revival.

To many, revival means lots of healings, deliverances, salvations, people getting baptized in water and also in the Spirit. That would be nice, but we have to work things backwards. If we believe revival is coming, or should come, what are we doing to prepare ourselves and to prepare God's people for it?

Another question we must ask is this: do we believe we deserve so-called revivals?

Have our ministries changed the temperature of our region?

Have all the neighbors in your area been invited to your church?

Have they heard the gospel?

Remember, we ought to be adding new believers to the church. Has your church met the needs of your community? The Word of God tells us to start with our Jerusalem first, correct? Reaching the homeless in our area, prison ministry, providing events for the community about drugs, the drugs that are killing our youth, and so on.

You see, I saw churches grow because TRUTH was preached and taught. I was amazed that people would come to hear God's truth. That is when I realized there is a HUGE GAP in the world, in our cities, a gap of God's truth, a gap of the Word of God as Jesus would preach it, with no fear of who we might offend or who might leave our churches.

Another HUGE GAP is that some, not all, ministers are good at creating a big name for themselves in their community, but they neglect those whom God sent to them to nurture and care for. These huge gaps are opportunities for others to fill, and God will work with you.

When I went to these churches and saw them grow, or when we had a radio program that reached four different states or provinces, and many followed us, they did not follow us because we had a compromised message. They followed us because we carried a message that made us UNPOPULAR. Many loved those messages, but others, including church leaders, did not receive them because the message challenged them to remove ear-tickling sermons and return to the Word of God.

These messages were loved by many and hated by others. My wife once said to me, "How in the world will you have friends with the messages you are teaching and preaching?" She understood the effectiveness of preaching truth, but her husband was not popular. Thank God she also saw that the minority in that region, including a few pastors, accepted the message I carried.

One day in that region, I was sitting in a restaurant when a man of God, known by most of the leaders, came in, knelt before me, and asked me to forgive the many leaders who were not accepting the message. I felt God showing me to continue in the direction He was leading me.

I prayed for those who did not accept me or my message. They were afraid that I would start a church in their city, but the Lord never called me to start a church there. He called me to hold a school of discipleship, where many came from different denominations to hear the truth of His Word as Jesus would teach it.

I saw that experience as a Jeremiah experience. Jeremiah was called to preach a message that would not be received. My call into ministry was not based on people receiving the message God placed in my heart, but on OBEDIENCE TO THE CALL.

These leaders were not my enemies; they were brothers. God was shaking their beliefs, and even those who did not like me told me they were listening to the messages. I may not have seen the fruit I wanted to see, but I know God sent me there to do His work, and one day I will discover how many lives were transformed in those four areas.

"Trust and obey, for there's no other way. To be happy in Jesus is to trust and obey."

Now, the most important thing I want to say, please never forget this: as I was obeying God in that region, that was a mini revival. When the disciples traveled, they did not travel to a denomination, but to a region. People came to hear them. That is what happened to us. People came from different denominations and churches, and I never bothered asking which church they were from.

I will never forget what one lady said to me: "Why do some pastors not like you here?" It is sad to hear such things when we believe there is ONE HEAVEN, not one for me and another for others. If we believe there is one heaven, we must do all we can to walk in unity, to see others and ourselves, in the process of becoming like Christ.

Some are more mature than we are, and perhaps we are more mature than others. If we are more mature, then we must show others what they are missing so they, too, can reach a higher level in their relationship with God.

Let Us Now Dig in Why Many Revivals Didn't Last.

What I am about to share now is what I believe the Lord has shown me over the past few years. If it makes sense to you, great. If not, that is fine as well.

ARE YOU READY?

Here it goes.

We read about the many revivals around the world, Azusa Street, the Welsh Revival, and so many others that took place across the globe: South Korea, Argentina, El Salvador, and others.

I had the privilege of witnessing the revival in Argentina and saw firsthand a mighty move of God, the hunger in God's people, the healings, the manifestations of demonic powers, and God delivering people from them. These are things many do not see in America and other parts of the world.

What the Lord shared with me was this: wherever He visited in a mighty way, churches that were in the hundreds became mega churches, and those churches missed the purpose of God in His visitation. Churches grew, and the main pastor became bigger. People's eyes were on the leadership, not on the purpose of God for that visitation.

So many of those moves came and went. Why?

You see, the Holy Spirit NEVER came to lift up a man, but to lift up JESUS alone. And if He is lifted up, He will draw all men unto Himself. Instead, man became greater, and what did we see in the past few years....

- The focus was on manifestations rather than on getting closer to God.
- Leaders failed to multiply themselves and make disciples. The purpose of God was never for leaders to become greater in the eyes of man, but for Jesus to be glorified.
- Then we saw churches going backwards instead of forward, and eventually that mighty visitation left.
- We saw deception enter the churches, where the Word of God no longer became a priority. I could spend pages describing the deceptions that have entered churches. In our time, we have seen many of these pastors deceived, leaving the faith and rejecting what they once believed.
- We now see many mega churches being exposed, pastors resigning, others going to prison, and the list goes on and on. Why? One of the reasons is that we take our eyes off Jesus and leave that place of prayer, our time with God. We abandon our priorities and confuse them. Then we neglect our children, and we have seen pastors' children

commit suicide, marriages break up because of adultery, spouses leaving marriages for the opposite sex, and now we see them leaving for the same sex.

The Word says that He is looking for a man to stand in the gap, not an army, but a simple man. A better world starts with you and me. It is about what we do for the Lord, what we do to advance the Kingdom of God, not our own. He is also looking for those with perfect hearts toward Him, that He might show Himself strong through them.

If you have made it this far in this book, please understand that God is speaking to you to make a difference where you are. Start with your relationship with God, then look after your family. If you don't, the Bible calls us worse than an unbeliever. We may shine in the world, but not at home.

Love your spouse. Love your children. Give them quality time to show them that you love them. And if you are single, learn to be complete in Christ before praying for a husband or a wife. I am in the process of writing a book on families, because the strength of a nation is determined by the strength of its families.

Now, here is the part the Lord revealed to me about His visitations.

I had the privilege, as I said, to witness a couple of revivals or visitations of God. The one in Argentina was held in a theater that seated 2,500 people, yet they accommodated over 100,000 attendees (before the pandemic). They had services nearly 22 hours a day to meet the crowds that came.

But one thing I noticed was that there were many pastors involved. The church was not built upon one man, but in the way I believe the Lord intended. If we commit to doing the same, I am sure the Lord will bless you with souls for His Kingdom. Your church might not grow to 100,000, but you will accept what God sends and understand that a visitation is meant to multiply ourselves, not to build everything around a person.

I also had the privilege of visiting the third or fourth largest church in the world, in El Salvador. At that time, they had between 300,000 and 400,000 people attending. Again, I saw many pastors working together. They did it God's way.

Years later, the main pastor got into moral problems and left the church, but the church continued to thrive. Why? Because it was not built on him, but on Christ. The good news is that the pastor was later restored and went elsewhere to start another work. Even in churches that are doing things right, situations like this may occur, but because the foundation is Christ, the churches endure.

Let us go back to Ezekiel 33:31-33 (New King James Version):

"So they come to you as people do, they sit before you as My people, and they hear your words, but they do not do them; for with their mouth they show much love, but their hearts pursue their own gain. Indeed, you are to them as a very lovely song of one who has a pleasant voice and can play well on an instrument; for they hear your words, but they do not do them. And when this comes to pass, surely it will come, then they will know that a prophet has been among them."

They come as God's people, but they do not do what they hear. With their mouths, they show much love, meaning they know how to talk Christian, but their hearts pursue other things, other gains.

They go to church, hear God's Word, but leave unchanged. They continue in the journey of hearing but not doing.

And when this comes to pass, SURELY IT WILL COME (I believe this is where we are), then they will know that a prophet has been among them.

1. This means that they refused to hear. They continue in their ways, in their sin, and when something drastic takes place, they will ponder and realize that a prophet was among them. But they never took it in; they rejected the Word, and by rejecting the Word, they were rejecting God and His blessings.

2. I believe that we are returning to the days of the Bible, where prophets spoke to governments, pulpits, and individuals, bringing the fear of God to the people and those in authority. Many of them died for it.

WE ARE GOING BACK TO THE DAYS OF THE BIBLE, WHERE PROPHETS AND GOD'S PEOPLE BROUGHT THE WORD OF GOD, AND BY DOING SO, THE FEAR OF GOD CAME. THOSE WHO OPPOSED THE WORD KILLED THOSE WHO SPOKE "THUS SAYS THE LORD!"

You see, what this world needs TODAY are those who will be the voice of God for the hour and be willing to pay the price, the ultimate price of serving Jesus.

These are the ones who will speak against the evil and wrong doctrines that have infiltrated so many churches, and against the many false gospels that people are embracing today. There is hardly any preaching on repentance. Many preachers fear declaring, "Thus says the Lord" because of fear of losing popularity. They have not learned from the Master Himself.

"Let this mind be in you which was also in Christ Jesus, who, being in the form of God, did not consider it robbery to be equal with God, but made Himself of no reputation, taking the form of a bondservant, and coming in the likeness of men."

You see, we want a reputation. We want to be loved by people, and in doing so, we can enter into a compromised gospel, a gospel of positive thinking, a gospel of convenience, a gospel that tickles the ears.

Let me tell you a true story so we can see what the call of God might entail at times.

Many years ago, I was called to a very unpopular call of God. The Lord asked me if I would accept it, and not knowing where it would take me, I said yes. The Lord sent me to a region where I had to fulfil a Jeremiah-type call. First, He gave me this scripture...

Exodus 3:7–10 (New King James Version)

"And the Lord said: 'I have surely seen the oppression of My people who are in Egypt, and have heard their cry because of their taskmasters, for I know their sorrows. So I have come down to deliver them out of the hand of the Egyptians, and to bring them up from that land to a good and large land, to a land flowing with milk and honey, to the place of the Canaanites and the Hittites and the Amorites and the Perizzites and the Hivites and the Jebusites. Now therefore, behold, the cry of the children of Israel has come to Me, and I have also seen the oppression with which the Egyptians oppress them. Come now, therefore, and I will send you to Pharaoh that you may bring My people, the children of Israel, out of Egypt."

What I understood from this is that He has heard the cry of the people in that region, and He wanted to rescue them. He was sending me to do something for Him.

He opened a door for the radio, where I would be speaking to three regions. It was a Christian radio station, and the reach was over 700,000 listeners.

Then the details came. He said:

1. You will be unpopular.
2. You will be rejected by many leaders, but accepted by some.
3. I want you to bring people back to prayer and preach a message of repentance, preach on living a holy life, you get the point. This was not a message to gain friends or popularity.

I accepted the call. I was on the radio twice a week, held a school of discipleship once a week, and led several evangelistic outreaches in the area.

Now, imagine an outsider coming in and shaking things up. Pastors were not happy that I was there, even though I tried to reach many of them. Only a couple responded, believing in the call of God upon my life, and became part of what I was doing.

Then I found out that some of those who did not accept me listened to the radio program every week, but they couldn't criticize it because it carried the bold Word of God.

One Saturday night, I was sitting at home and got a call from one of them. I had attended his church for a while, but left after discovering that he was entertaining the Masons and probably had ties to them. He was a very popular pastor in that area. The reason he didn't accept me was because of the message I carried. He liked me as a person, but he was afraid of the message.

You have to understand that many of these leaders who have compromised the true gospel of the Lord are good people. They started well, but at some point in their ministry, they took a detour. Some of them don't know their way back unless they hear the voice of God for themselves.

So, on that Saturday night, this pastor called me and asked a question that made me almost fall off my chair. I couldn't believe it, and it never happened again. He said, "Brother John, I had a busy week and I have no word to preach tomorrow morning. Do you have a word that I could preach?"

WOW! A person who rejects me was asking me for a Word of God to preach on Sunday!

You see, I learned something important here: even though they are afraid of you or reject you in front of their peers, they can respect your calling. He respected my calling, even though he didn't like me among his peers.

I told him, "Give me 30 minutes; I will ask the Lord and see what He says." The Lord gave me a word for him to preach the next day. He was thankful and preached on the passage and details I provided.

I would never use this against him. The Lord was showing me that if His people would only do what He tells us to do, we would enter a place of revelation. We would enter into a seat as friends of God. According to the Word of God, Jesus said, "I no longer call you servants but friends; I will not hold anything back."

Do you want that?

If you do, you have to let Him fully into your life and ministry. He doesn't bless churches of man or homes of man, but churches of God, where the Holy Spirit is Lord over the church and its people. Only then will He share His revelations, things we do not know, not to judge, but to understand what time it is with God. You enter into a place in God that many pray for but never experience. That is what it means to understand our God.

Jeremiah 9:24 (King James Version)

"But let him that glorieth glory in this, that he understandeth and knoweth me, that I am the Lord which exercise lovingkindness, judgment, and righteousness, in the earth: for in these things I delight, saith the Lord."

Not only knowing Him, but UNDERSTANDING HIM, that takes intentional steps on our part to reach that place in God. Paul reached that level, as did other disciples, through obedience, devotion, and continual pursuit of God's presence and Word...

James 1:2-4 (New King James Version)

Profiting from Trials

"My brethren, count it all joy when you fall into various trials, knowing that the testing of your faith produces [a]patience. But let patience have its perfect work, that you may be [b]perfect and complete, lacking nothing."

Paul understood this deeply; he knew how to enter that place in God. The real question remains: Do you want that?

How to Know if the Holy Spirit is in Your Midst?

What are the signs that the Holy Spirit is present in your home, your life, your church, or your ministry? Let me explain it this way.

I have a friend who is an intercessor from Kenya. Many leaders in her area are somewhat afraid of her because of her deep connection with God, yet she is a wonderful lady. My family and I are on her prayer list. I'm not afraid of her, but I'm grateful to have her on my side.

Many people respect her greatly. She left her home country with just a few dollars in her pocket and two children, all in the hope of giving them a better life. Today, both of her children have completed university, are employed, and are thriving. All of this is the result of her faith in God and her constant prayers. God provided for her every need, and most importantly, for the needs of her children.

She could write an entire book about her journey of faith with the Lord.

But my point here is this, I often tell people, "If she were coming to visit your home for dinner, what would you do?" Many who know her would probably make sure they are right with the Lord. They would pray and prepare themselves for such a visitation, in case she sees something in them, all because they know she is a woman of God, an intercessor, and someone who walks closely with the Lord. In other words, they would prepare for her visit.

This is very similar for us. How do we know if the Holy Spirit is in our lives...?

A) You wouldn't be the same person you were a year ago.
B) If there was sin in your life, the Holy Spirit would show you and help you get rid of it.
C) You would desire to know the God of the Bible, feeling a deep hunger to know Him. You'd want to spend a lot of time with Him, in His presence.
D) You would allow Him to convict, rebuke, and correct you. You wouldn't want to grieve Him.
E) You would fear allowing sin into your life, knowing that it would separate you from Him, something we desperately need today. Allowing sin would give the devil a foothold in your life and could blind you to the wrong you've allowed in.
F) You would display the fruit of the Spirit to those around you, your spouse, your children, your parents. The opposite of this is rebellion, and the Bible calls rebellion the sin of witchcraft.

1 Samuel 15:23 (New King James Version)

"For rebellion is as the sin of witchcraft, and stubbornness is as iniquity and idolatry. Because you have rejected the word of the Lord, He also has rejected you from being king."

This is the reason chaos happens in families. The head of the home should be the protector, the guide, and the provider. Instead, he grieves the Holy Spirit by rebelling against the Word of God, which could bless his home. Then, we have children rebelling against their parents because they don't want to do what is right. They leave their homes, the very place that is supposed to be their covering, and many end up sleeping in empty buildings in the cities, all because they rebelled against the rules of their homes.

I see this all the time. Our homes are broken. Where the Holy Spirit is grieved, the blessings of God are broken, and they are NOT there. Believing in God is not enough. It's LIVING WHAT WE BELIEVE that makes all the difference.

James 1:22-25 (New King James Version)

"But be doers of the word, and not hearers only, deceiving yourselves. For if anyone is a hearer of the word and not a doer, he is like a man observing his natural face in a mirror; for he observes himself, goes away, and immediately forgets what kind of man he was. But he who looks into the perfect law of liberty and continues in it, and is not a forgetful hearer but a doer of the work, this one will be blessed in what he does."

You see, when you are ONLY a hearer of the word and not a doer, YOU DECEIVE YOURSELF. You're not deceiving your parents, your spouse, your pastor, your friends, or your siblings; you're deceiving YOURSELF.

That is why many are not experiencing the full blessings of our God. You see, we are complete in Him; in Him, we have everything. We have everything that heaven has to offer. Yet, instead, we often experience the bad of this world. Most of what we do feels like sand slipping through our fingers, missed opportunities, closed doors, and a failure to mature in life. Instead of growing, we end up growing in hate, resentment, and blaming others for our misery.

I'm in the process of writing a book in 2026 titled "The Strength of a Nation," which focuses on how strong our homes truly are.

Signs that the Holy Spirit is in our churches.

1. Is the Gospel of Repentance Preached?

We will dedicate one chapter of this book to the true gospel. Jesus' first message was, "Repent, for the kingdom of God has come unto you." Recently, a group of people took me out for lunch, and we started discussing the Bible. They asked me many questions, and I shared with them the things we teach in discipleship, end times, the true gospel, and more.

Their response was striking: "We do not hear messages or teachings on this anymore. We don't hear them in our churches." One of them even said, "I grew up hearing these teachings, but we don't hear them anymore." This is a HUGE PROBLEM, and it raises the question: Is the Holy Spirit still present??

2. Is There a Love for the Lost? Jesus left the 99 to search for the one lost sheep. Shouldn't a sign of the Holy Spirit in our midst be a love for the lost, just like Jesus? Are we actively adding to the church, weekly, monthly, daily?

Acts 2:47 (New King James Version)

"Praising God and having favor with all the people. And the Lord added to the church daily those who were being saved."

3. Is Jesus Lifted Up or Man?

John 12:32 (New King James Version)

"And I, if I am lifted up from the earth, will draw all peoples to Myself."

You see, if we belong to a church led by man, we will not experience the fullness of God. In such churches, man dictates what happens, often seeking to control everything. They place people in positions they can control, grieving the Holy Spirit in the process. Sadly, we see many churches today where these leaders fall into sin. We must understand that the devil is looking for carnal leaders he can use to infiltrate ministries. At the right moment, he brings them down, and in the aftermath, God's people are hurt. They scatter without a shepherd, and many leave the faith or join different sects, rebelling against what they once knew as the true God. They allowed themselves to be under leadership where man became the lord of the church.

We know the Holy Spirit is present when there is a soul-winning church, where Jesus is lifted up, and where there is humility to understand that it is not by might, nor by power, nor by the arm of flesh, but BY THE HOLY SPIRIT.

4. **Another Sign that the Holy Spirit is Present or Not**

   A) Is there a dedicated time for prayer throughout the week? Do the leaders of the church attend these prayer meetings, or do they skip them?

I have encountered some churches where the leadership does not attend prayer meetings. The reason they are called leaders is that they lead. We cannot lead others closer to God if we, ourselves, are not there. We cannot give what we do not have.

Should We Have a Passion for Prayer as Leaders? Do We Recognize that Prayer Could Be Our Highest Calling?

We've quoted this for years: a prayerless church is a powerless church. But why do we, as leaders, sometimes detour from prayer?

- Too busy?
- Sin?
- Running on empty?

There could be many reasons, but the truth is, the sign that the Holy Spirit is in our midst is that we are a church of prayer, where prayer is both taught and practiced. The Bible says...

1 Thessalonians 5:16-18 (New King James Version)

"Rejoice always, Pray without ceasing, In everything give thanks; for this is the will of God in Christ Jesus for you."

What about Fasting?

As mentioned earlier, we organized an all-night prayer meeting and invited local pastors to join us. It was a great opportunity to show God's people that we can unite in prayer, and perhaps we could do this twice a year. One pastor came, along with another retired pastor, and we gave them sessions to bring scriptures and guide us on what we should pray for during their time. It was powerful! We went from 7 PM to 7 AM, and for those who remained, we went on a prayer walk in the city.

Prayer creates momentum; it paves the way for God's will and serves as spiritual warfare. We don't battle against flesh and blood, but against the powers of darkness. Through prayer, we can disrupt the plans of Satan in our cities, our families, and beyond. In JESUS' NAME, we have authority, and with fasting, even more so. Look at this story in the Bible...

Matthew 17:14-21 (New King James Version)

The Boy Is Healed

And when they had come to the multitude, a man came to Him, kneeling down to Him and saying, "Lord, have mercy on my son, for he is an epileptic and suffers severely; for he often falls into the fire and often into the water. So I brought him to Your disciples, but they could not cure him." Then Jesus answered and said, "O faithless and perverse generation, how long shall I be with you? How long shall I bear with you? Bring him here to Me." And Jesus rebuked the demon, and it came out of him; and the child was cured from that very hour. Then the disciples came to Jesus privately and said, "Why could we not cast it out?" So Jesus said to them, "Because of your unbelief; for assuredly, I say to you, if you have faith as a mustard seed, you will say to this mountain, 'Move from here to there,' and it will move; and nothing will be impossible for you. However, this kind does not go out except by prayer and fasting."

Here, Jesus reveals the importance of fasting and prayer. What the Lord showed me about this is that we are to live a life of fasting and prayer so that we are ready to do His work effectively. We must be prepared to pray for people and even cast out demons in JESUS' NAME, just as we did in Mexico City with Lupita. There is power in His name.

Is Your Church Ready for such Things?

Are We Ready for the Lord to Add More New Christians to Our Church?

Many churches pray for revival, but often forget to work backwards. What do we need to have a revival in our midst?

- **Prepare God's People for It (Ephesians 4:11)**

We need to prepare God's people for the revival we pray for. Revival begins in our hearts and our readiness to embrace new believers.

- **Train Them in Evangelism and Follow-Up**

What do we have ready for anyone who might come to Jesus this week? Do we have materials for them, a Bible for them? Why would God send more people when we are not ready to receive them?

- **Learn to Disciple Them**

New converts need spiritual nourishment, just like newborn babies need milk. The Bible teaches us this truth. The mistake many make is throwing new believers into services before they are mature enough to understand what is being preached, and as a result, we lose them. The Lord wants to trust you with new converts, so we must be prepared. There should be three levels of discipleship:

A) New Converts Class (Milk)

This is where new believers are taught the basics of their faith, the foundation they need to grow spiritually.

B) Soft Discipleship

This can take place in a Sunday school class or small group setting, where topics like the life of Paul, prayer, or Christian living are discussed. This level builds a deeper understanding.

C) Deep Discipleship

This is for the more mature believers. Topics here may include: "I die daily," "For me to live is Christ," and "Though the outer man perishes, he is renewed day by day." I call this deep discipleship because it teaches us what it takes to follow Him, where we decrease truly, and He increases in us.

Luke 14:25-27

Living Bible

"Great crowds were following Him. He turned around and addressed them, saying, Anyone who wants to be my follower must love me far more than his own father, mother, wife, children, brothers, or sisters, yes, more than his own life; otherwise, he cannot be my disciple. And no one can be my disciple who does not carry his own cross and follow me."

There's a cost to being a follower of Christ.

The question should never be, "Are you a Christian?" but rather, "Are you a follower of Christ?"

To be a follower of Christ is to be Christlike, not merely by name but by life, reflecting who He truly is.

We have people who have never read the Bible. How can you truly know Him if you don't read about Him? I remember the first time I met my wife; we talked for hours. The next time, we spoke for hours again. Why? Because we both wanted to know everything about each other.

How much do you know about God? Many claim to love God, but do they truly know Him?

Imagine, Moses, who knew the power of God, and after witnessing it, he said...

Exodus 33:13 (New King James Version)

"Now therefore, I pray, if I have found grace in Your sight, show me now Your way, that I may know You and that I may find grace in Your sight. And consider that this nation is Your people."

John 17:3 (New King James Version)

"And this is eternal life, that they may know You, the only true God, and Jesus Christ whom You have sent."

Before I share the True Gospel of Jesus Christ, I want to direct this message to the corrupt judges and politicians. I see this not only as pure evil but as people fulfilling the will of evil, working against the will of God for Americans and all people around the world.

Corrupt Judges

I fear for those judges who claim to be Christians but have fallen into participating in the evil they are now part of. If these judges are NOT FOLLOWERS OF CHRIST and participate in evil agendas, abusing their power to hinder the good of a nation, their deeds are set to bring destruction upon America. These are strong words, but this is how the world sees them. They have NO FEAR OF GOD, no concern for what their families think, and are blind to reality and common sense. Perhaps they once knew the truth, but now, out of hatred toward others or being forced to do the will of others, they have placed themselves in a very dangerous position before God.

My heart goes out to those who are abusing their power to do what a JUST JUDGE would do. Instead, they appear to be indifferent to what America thinks and are willing to sacrifice their reputation for the agenda they serve.

- Are we a politician first or a follower of Christ first?
- Are we a leader first or a follower of Christ first?
- Are you a preacher first or a follower of Christ first?

You see, this is the issue, many place their calling above their faith. Shouldn't faith, your relationship with God, come first, before your position? I know many in this world who have left their positions because it was contrary to their beliefs. They chose to follow Christ fully, rather than compromise their faith and their message for what was offered to them. I know musicians who turned down million-dollar contracts because they went against their faith and relationship with God.

- Is God happy with your relationship with Him?
- Are you righteous before God and others?
- Righteousness means being in the right standing with God.
- Are you in the right standing with God, or is your heart filled with worldly things, and have you been contaminated by the cares of this world?
- You see, what this book is all about is this: Are you ALL IN for God or not?
- Are you a true believer or an unbelieving believer?
- A form of godliness but denying His power?
- YOU SEE, GOD IS COMING BACK FOR A HOLY CHURCH, A HOLY PEOPLE. We don't become holy by ourselves, but we become holy when we hang around with God and spend a lot of time with Him. People say tell me who your friends are, and I will tell you who you are.
- Is God your close friend?

My prayer for this book is that it would minister to someone, and that person would have a positive outcome and become a true follower of Christ. For when you become a true follower of Christ, you receive all that heaven offers, and you will be COMPLETE IN HIM.

Please pray for judges and politicians, because some of them will go down in history as the worst of our time.

You might ask, "You say you're a follower of Christ, are you saying that other religions are spiritually in trouble?"

I want to answer this in the best way possible, with TRUTH and with LOVE for people, people from all walks of life.

I'd like to quote a couple of scriptures and take it from there.

You see, we have different religions, some that believe...

1) They believe that Jesus came and is coming back, but they do not believe He died and rose again. If they did believe that He died and rose again, that would mean He is God.

John 1:1 (New King James Version)

The Eternal Word

"In the beginning was the Word, and the Word was with God, and the Word was God."

The Word Becomes Flesh

"And the Word became flesh and dwelt among us, and we beheld His glory, the glory as of the only begotten of the Father, full of grace and truth."

You see, here it tells us that THE WORD is JESUS. THE WORD BECAME FLESH AND DWELT AMONG US (Jesus did that).

Then, we have a scripture in the Bible that says, "I am the FIRST and the LAST, the beginning and the end." If you ask who that is, many so-called people of God would tell you it is Jehovah God. Let's now read a scripture with those words in the New Testament...

Revelation 1:17-18 (King James Version)

"And when I saw him, I fell at his feet as dead. And he laid his right hand upon me, saying unto me, Fear not; I am the first and the last: I am he that liveth, and was dead; and, behold, I am alive for evermore, Amen; and have the keys of hell and of death."

You see, the answers are not found anywhere else but in the scriptures, in the Bible. That's the reason the enemy keeps people from the scriptures and prayer, so they become powerless in their spiritual walk and are drawn into a worldly life.

Jesus is the Alpha and the Omega. Jesus is the First and the Last. Jesus is the ONLY ONE that DIED, the ONLY ONE that was DEAD, and is ALIVE FOREVERMORE.

Praise God!

Acts 4:12 (New King James Version)

"Nor is there salvation in any other, for there is no other name under heaven given among men by which we must be saved."

Have you ever thought about whether that scripture is true?

Or how about this one...

John 14:6 (King James Version)

"Jesus saith unto him, I am the way, the truth, and the life: no man cometh unto the Father, but by me."

And then there's this scripture. We don't preach about it much, but let it speak to you and see where it takes you. I challenge you, in the name of Jesus, to examine your faith and ask yourself: Are you in the right place with God? Do you have THE TRUTH, or something that might look like the truth and sound like the truth, but isn't? Or perhaps a faith that was taught to you but you've never had a chance to question or search for yourself to see if you are truly in the faith?

Look at this, this is what Jesus said...

John 14:9 (King James Version)

"Jesus saith unto him, 'Have I been so long time with you, and yet hast thou not known me, Philip? He that hath seen me hath seen the Father; and how sayest thou then, Show us the Father?'"

Are you getting it?

Let us pray this prayer together. It could be the most important prayer you will ever pray. I prayed this once with a friend I bumped into on a train. I was a Christian, and he followed a different faith. I asked him, "Let us put all of our beliefs in our back pockets and pray to our Maker, asking Him to reveal truth to us and show us the way to TRUE SALVATION." He agreed, and we prayed.

I believe that God is bound to answer such a sincere prayer. The Bible says...

1 John 5:14-15 (New King James Version)

"Now this is the confidence that we have in Him, that if we ask anything according to His will, He hears us. And if we know that He hears us, whatever we ask, we know that we have the petitions that we have asked of Him."

IS THERE ONE HEAVEN?

Ephesians 4:5-6 (King James Version)

"One Lord, one faith, one baptism, One God and Father of all, who is above all, and through all, and in you all."

Matthew 6:10 (New King James Version)

"Your kingdom come. Your will be done, on earth as it is in heaven."

People often view heaven as a place we go after we die.

We say things like this:

- He or she is in a better place
- He or she is at peace now
- He or she is not suffering anymore
- Hope he or she made it to heaven

Rarely does anyone talk about hell after death. The Bible does speak about hell, but this portion is focused on heaven. The Bible also speaks of a third heaven, but here I want to concentrate on what most people believe, heaven.

My question to people for the past few years has been this: is there a heaven for Christians and another heaven for people of other religions? I like to believe that if you live unto God, you will go where God is.

2 Corinthians 5:8 (King James Version)

"We are confident, I say, and willing rather to be absent from the body, and to be present with the Lord."

Of course, the Bible also talks about judgments and other related matters. But my point here is this: we MUST all get along in this world if we want to go to that place. We MUST seek and make sure we have the TRUTH to get there, as we have written in this book.

The Bible also says, ONE LORD, ONE FAITH, ONE BAPTISM. It does not speak of two or three, but ONE. This topic alone could be another book. What I want to focus on here is that earth is our opportunity to get to know our Creator and to understand that one of our purposes here on earth is to find out about Him, know Him, love Him, and live unto Him.

My testimony is like this scripture:

Acts 4:20 (New King James Version)

"For we cannot but speak the things which we have seen and heard."

You see, I was LOST, but He picked me up. I was a no-good sinner, but He died for me and rose from the dead to give me life. Because He lives, I live today.

I am not the person I was when Jesus came into my life. He is real to me. The message of this book exists because I am a follower of Christ, and I would never follow someone who is not real, someone who does not make us better people.

The Holy Spirit is with me and lives in me. He convicts me, rebukes me, corrects me, and encourages me. I know He lives, and I am blessed, because the Bible says:

John 20:29 (New King James Version)

"Jesus said to him, 'Thomas, because you have seen Me, you have believed. Blessed are those who have not seen and yet have believed.'"

That is ME. I have never seen Him, but I know He is there. He answers prayers. He brings me through hard times in life. He has given me His Word, His Name, and His blood shed on Calvary is there for me.

1 John 1:7 (King James Version)

"But if we walk in the light, as He is in the light, we have fellowship one with another, and the blood of Jesus Christ His Son cleanseth us from all sin."

He is the love of my life. I am complete in Him. You can have this as well, just as many millions all over the world have experienced. Jesus is waiting for you. Come as you are. He has the power to change you.

He transformed me and is still doing it. Come to Him TODAY, for TODAY IS YOUR DAY FOR SALVATION, salvation from your past life and salvation from living a life without Him. He knows your yesterdays, and He knows your tomorrows, and He knows your tomorrows are better with Him.

Blessings.

1. Then you have others who are still waiting for the Messiah. The good news is that the Messiah has already come. His name is Jesus, the Anointed One. Many of those who were waiting for the Messiah grew tired of waiting and decided to search for themselves to see whether He had already come or not. Many discovered that He had indeed already come, and they embraced Jesus as their Lord, Savior, and Messiah. This is wonderful to see, how millions decided to search for themselves and found that the God of the Bible is the real God, the true God. Praise His name.

2. Then you have those who chose to become atheists, some who were always that way, perhaps brought up like that, and others who once believed but chose atheism because of hurt or bad experiences in their lives. I believe this group makes up the majority: offended people. Perhaps their trust was placed in man and not in God, so when something happened, they abandoned their beliefs and chose to leave the faith. Maybe what they had was only belief without living out what they believed, what we call unbelieving believers.

Psalm 14:1a (New King James Version)

"The fool has said in his heart, there is no God."

Matthew 24:10-13 (English Standard Version)

"And then many will fall away[a] and betray one another and hate one another. And many false prophets will arise and lead many astray. And because lawlessness will be increased, **the love of many will grow cold.** But the one who endures to the end will be saved."

Matthew 7:24-27 (New Living Translation)

"Anyone who listens to my teaching and follows it is wise, like a person who builds a house on solid rock. Though the rain comes in torrents and the floodwaters rise and the winds beat against that house, it won't collapse because it is built on bedrock. But anyone who hears my teaching and doesn't obey it is foolish, like a person who builds a house on sand. When the rains and floods come and the winds beat against that house, it will collapse with a mighty crash."

Conclusion

The True Gospel of the Lord Jesus Christ

I want to conclude this book by sharing the TRUE GOSPEL of the Lord Jesus Christ from the Word of God.

We all believe that the Gospel is GOOD NEWS. But what is good news in the Gospel? Yes, He is a loving God, that is good news. Jesus comes and says:

"Son/Daughter, you are going in the wrong way in life; this is the way you should take."

Is that good news? Of course it is. Knowing that He is a loving God is good news. Knowing that He is a holy God, and that He calls us to be holy, is good news. He calls us to follow Him and leave a life of sin, that is good news. So, in order to understand the TRUE GOSPEL, we must also understand what good news truly is.

We also have to understand some of the wrong gospels.

– The Gospel of prosperity. Lately, we have witnessed many of these teachers who have so-called repented for teaching wrongly on tithing. These are preachers who have based their entire business on prosperity, where many of them in North America are millionaires and some even billionaires.

I heard a wonderful story about John Wesley and his accomplishments.

- He started a denomination
- He sponsored many missionaries
- Started a Bible College and did many of those things with the money God provided for him
- When he died it is said that he only had $300 or so to his name, he invested all his money in the needs of Gods kingdom and his basic needs. He stored his reaches in heaven.....

Matthew 6:19-21 (King James Version")

"Lay not up for yourselves treasures upon earth, where moth and rust doth corrupt, and where thieves break through and steal. But lay up for yourselves treasures in heaven, where neither moth nor rust doth corrupt, and where thieves do not break through nor steal. For where your treasure is, there will your heart be also."

James 1:17 (New King James Version)

"Every good gift and every perfect gift is from above, and comes down from the Father of lights, with whom there is no variation or shadow of turning."

We give out of what God gives unto us. All that we have belongs to God.

He gives to us to test us and to see what we will do with what He gives. The question is, "Have we passed the test?"

Of course, God wants us to live a life of wealth, but we must understand where wealth comes from and the purpose of wealth.

Deuteronomy 8:18 (New King James Version)

"And you shall remember the LORD your God, for it is He who gives you power to get wealth, that He may establish His covenant which He swore to your fathers, as it is this day."

He gives us the power to get wealth for a purpose. So the question is not for who, but for what purpose? When we realize this, we will never misunderstand the power of wealth. His blessings have a purpose, and when we understand that purpose, we will never lack anything, knowing that all I have belongs to the King of kings, the LORD of my life and the Lord of my belongings.

Please read the Parable of the Talents found in, Matthew 25:14–30.

The True Gospell

The Lord revealed 5 steps of the True Gospel

1. What was Jesus FIRST MESSAGE?

Matthew 4:17

"From that time Jesus began to preach and say, 'Repent, for the kingdom of heaven is at hand.'"

Yes, that was His first message, a message we do not hear much anymore in our pulpits, afraid of losing popularity, afraid of losing congregants in the church. But Jesus came, and His first message is exactly what is needed today: REPENTANCE, turning from our ways to His.

When we do that and embrace His Word, He translates us from darkness into light.

Romans 6:14–23 (New King James Version)

"For sin shall not have dominion over you, for you are not under law but under grace."

From Slaves of Sin to Slaves of God

"What then? Shall we sin because we are not under law but under grace? Certainly not! Do you not know that to whom you present yourselves slaves to obey, you are that one's slaves whom you obey, whether of sin leading to death, or of obedience leading to righteousness? But God be thanked that though you were slaves of sin, yet you obeyed from the heart that form of doctrine to which you were delivered. And having been set free from sin, you became slaves of righteousness. I speak in human terms because of the weakness of your flesh. For just as you presented your members as slaves of uncleanness, and of lawlessness leading to more lawlessness, so now present your members as slaves of righteousness for holiness. For when you were slaves of sin, you were free in regard to righteousness. What fruit did you have then in the things of which you are now ashamed? For the end of those things is death. But now having been set free from sin, and having become slaves of God, you have your fruit to holiness, and the end, everlasting life. For the wages of sin is death, but the gift of God is eternal life in Christ Jesus our Lord."

A very powerful truth is found here: whoever we submit our members to, we become their servants, sin, which leads to evil and death, or righteousness, which leads to God. We cannot submit to God and to sin. There is only one Master.

John the Baptist's first message was also a gospel of repentance. This brings us to the first message of Peter as he came out of the upper room and preached the gospel of Jesus Christ.

Acts 2:38 (New King James Version)

"Then Peter said to them, 'Repent, and let every one of you be baptized in the name of Jesus Christ for the remission of sins; and you shall receive the gift of the Holy Spirit.'"

Here we see Peter, who the day before had denied Christ three times, now standing boldly. He went to the upper room, the Holy Spirit came, and he became a new creature.

Jesus said, "Tarry in Jerusalem, and I will send the Comforter to you," the Holy Spirit. The purpose of God was that the Holy Spirit would now dwell in us. In the old covenant, the Holy Spirit came upon people, and people continued in sin. But now He said He would dwell in us, to help us, to convict us, to minister to us, to lead us into all truth, and to tell us what is yet to come.

Ezekiel 37:14 (English Standard Version)

"And I will put my Spirit within you, and you shall live, and I will place you in your own land. Then you shall know that I am the LORD; I have spoken, and I will do it, declares the LORD."

Praise God. He came to dwell in us by His Spirit, to help us, to transform us, and to convict us.

Peter preached, and they came to him and asked, "What must we do to get saved?" This was his answer: Repent and be baptized in the name of Jesus, and receive the free gift of the Holy Spirit, yes, a free gift. Come as you are, turn your life over to Him, and let Him make you the person He has called you to be. Praise God.

Baptism is very important because when we go under the water, not sprinkled with water, but, as in the Bible, immersed in the water, it has meaning. When we go under, we bury the old life, and when we come out, we receive the new life.

Romans 6:4 (English Standard Version)

"We were buried therefore with him by baptism into death, in order that, just as Christ was raised from the dead by the glory of the Father, we too might walk in newness of life."

1. He is coming back, praise God

He is coming back to take us one day soon, He is the groom and we are His bride, He will come in an hour we have no clue in, only the Father Knows, so we have to be ready,it could be today, a year from now, we do not know, but if we read the parable of the ten virgins we would understand how we ought to live our lives ready, 5 of those virgins we ready, the other ones were not, they probably said we will get ready at another time, then the invitation came, they were called to be with the groom, caught them unprepared as many people are today, and it ook them time to get ready but when they finally got their act together the door was shut and it was too late for them.

Matthew 25 (New International Version)

The Parable of the Ten Virgins

"At that time the kingdom of heaven will be like ten virgins who took their lamps and went out to meet the bridegroom. Five of them were foolish and five were wise. The foolish ones took their lamps but did not take any oil with them. The wise ones, however, took oil in jars along with their lamps. The bridegroom was a long time in coming, and they all became drowsy and fell asleep. At midnight the cry rang out: 'Here's the bridegroom! Come out to meet him!' 'Then all the virgins woke up and trimmed their lamps. The foolish ones said to the wise, 'Give us some of your oil; our lamps are going out.' 'No,' they replied, 'there may not be enough for both us and you. Instead, go to those who sell oil and buy some for yourselves.' But while they were on their way to buy the oil, the bridegroom arrived. The virgins who were ready went in with him to the wedding banquet. And the door was shut. Later the others also came. 'Lord, Lord,' they said, 'open the door for us!' But he replied, 'Truly I tell you, I don't know you.' Therefore keep watch, because you do not know the day or the hour."

Have You Turned Your Life Over to God?

TODAY IS THE DAY OF SALVATION

If you are not sure, pray this prayer with me:

Dear God,

I know I am a sinner and I need forgiveness. I now decide to be a follower of Christ and to leave a life of sin behind. Lord, save me. I am willing, by God's grace, to follow Him and obey Him for the rest of my life. Be the LORD OF MY LIFE, I pray, in the name of Jesus. Amen.

If you prayed that prayer and meant it, write to me at author@BestsellersbyJohnaAlexander.com, and I will send you a note and material to help you grow properly in the new life that God has provided for you and for me.

Lord, bless them, I pray, in the name of Jesus. Reveal Yourself to them and meet all of their needs, I pray, in the name of Jesus. May this book be blessed by You, as You have touched the readers and caused them to return back to You and serve You until You return for us. Amen.

John A. Alexander

www.ingramcontent.com/pod-product-compliance
Lightning Source LLC
Chambersburg PA
CBHW052120030426
42335CB00025B/3063